22 and Single

a coming of age story... in progress

KATIE KIESLER

WESTBOW
PRESS
A DIVISION OF THOMAS NELSON

WestBow Press books may be ordered through booksellers or by contacting:

WestBow Press
A Division of Thomas Nelson
1663 Liberty Drive
Bloomington, IN 47403
www.westbowpress.com
1-(866) 928-1240

Because of the dynamic nature of the Internet, any web addresses or links contained in this book may have changed since publication and may no longer be valid. The views expressed in this work are solely those of the author and do not necessarily reflect the views of the publisher, and the publisher hereby disclaims any responsibility for them.

Any people depicted in stock imagery provided by Thinkstock are models, and such images are being used for illustrative purposes only.

Certain stock imagery © Thinkstock.

ISBN: 978-1-4497-5646-8 (sc)
ISBN: 978-1-4497-5647-5 (e)

Library of Congress Control Number: 2012910610

Printed in the United States of America

WestBow Press rev. date: 07/17/2012

You did it: you changed wild lament
    into whirling dance;
You ripped off my black mourning band
    and decked me with wildflowers.
I'm about to burst with song;
    I can't keep quiet about you.
GOD, my God,
    I can't thank you enough.

–Psalm 30:11–12

"The Message"

Prologue

In 8th grade English, my teacher Mr. O made us journal for the first five minutes of every class period. Since then, I've never stopped. I wouldn't say that it's an addiction, but maybe. Even when I'm not journaling, my mind dictates to itself. I don't know if this has always been the case and Mr. O just tapped into an already pulsating line, or if he is the one who is responsible for my never-ending self-talk radio. Regardless, I can't turn it off, and I don't really want to because, sometimes, God comes on the line.

I realized somewhere along the way that thoughts are insignificant unless you allow someone else to interpret their meaning. So, I started publishing some of my thoughts on a blog called "Katie's Journal." Sometimes I feel like a narcissist and am afraid other people probably think so too. I'm hoping they hear God through my words and not me . . . It freaks me out to know that other people are reading my thoughts.

Writing a blog, or attempting to, made me realize that I'm terrified of being known. (Writing a blog is about as much self-disclosure as one person can take . . .) But I do want to be known. I want to be noticed, and I especially want to be found, and it's my dream to be discovered.

I think I just want to have a voice. I want to have a voice that gives other people a voice. I think that means that I want to be a microphone. I want to help other people's stories to be so loud that they can't be ignored. I want to give God a voice too—not because He needs me, but because I need Him. And if I know how much I need Him, maybe other people don't know how awesome it is to know Him and that their lives could be microphones too.

Anyway, I'm writing this because I want more than anything for my life to count. I want to be real. The only way I know how to do that is for the Lord to turn my plethora of weaknesses into strength, my mess into His message. In the past, every time I'd begin to write something that others might read, I would say what I thought was "right" and "proper" and ultimately "annoying." We don't get to edit life like I can a blog or a book. It just comes out and creates a personal narrative that we don't always want to take credit for writing.

This book is simply a collection of streaming thoughts as recorded and reworded and analyzed in the journal of a 22-year-old, single girl.

♥ ♥ ♥ ♥ ♥

Part 1

Unmarried

October 30, 2011

This past weekend I was surrounded by adorable Christian married couples.

I am single and it has never been so clearly visible.

This experience caused me to feel like I was lacking something, someone. I realized later that it was as if Satan had handed me a platter labeled "Everything You Don't Have." I've attempted to create a visual to show you just what I mean.

God has given me so much, yet I so easily become like a spoiled child—fixated on the one thing I haven't received . . . yet. It's so frustrating to see and know my own selfish nature.

It doesn't help that on the car ride home, I had a day-mare. This thought popped into my head of me being asked to sit on a relationship panel. You know, there's the one adorable married couple, the cute engaged couple, and the single female and the single male.

I never in my life wanted to be the single girl on the relationship panel. I wanted to be in one of the first two couples, spewing out Godly wisdom to all the pitiful (although I'd never admit to such an awful mindset) desperate single people who were hanging on my every knowledgeable word. In this vision, I am the pitiful desperate single girl, on display, no less.

Humbling.

In my day-mare, I couldn't get past my introduction. What would I say? Each couple would give a charming intro:

"Hi, I'm Mark and this is my wife and better half, Grace. We've been married for twenty magnificent years and have five amazing children."

"Hi, I'm Kristopher and this is my beautiful fiancée, Emily. I'm the most blessed man in the world."

And then it'd be my turn:

"Hi, I'm Katie and I'm single. I've been single for years . . . ."

AHHH.

I then tried to reword my introduction to make it sound less like I was on a dating show and more like I was in control and proud.

"Hi, I'm Katie and I'm unmarried and not dating."

Ugh . . . that sounded even more like a desperate dating show contestant!

"Hi, I'm Katie."

Yikes. I want to throw up just thinking about it. Clearly, this was a traumatic day for me. Trust me, I know how silly it is. I cry/ran/prayed about it. (P.S. If you see me jogging, feel free to stop me. If you see me cry/running/praying, let me be.)

I sat on a park swing after running until I could feel how out of shape I was in my lungs, thighs, and shins. I didn't come to any revelations. I tried making some deals with God, as if I were talking to my dad.

"But God, I just want someone . . . I don't want to be alone . . . please don't make me . . ."

All of this sounded like a stupid cop-out.

"For I know the plans I have for you," this is the Lord's declaration. "Plans to prosper you, not to harm you, plans to give you a future and a hope . . ." is all that came to mind.

I never did get to tie up this experience with a nice neat bow. I didn't feel all of sudden content or like I knew why God gave me this stunning gift of singleness. All I felt was God telling me to write about it on my blog, which I was at first excited about. Then, I realized I'd have to confront and deal with my feelings again. I wouldn't be able to shove them further down inside my secret inner singleness hatred box.

Something else did happen tonight though. I had the opportunity to make dinner for six college girlfriends. While I was preparing, it hit me: This is why I'm single. I can love on my fellow single ladies. I won't always get to do this if I do one day meet "Mr. Adorable Christian Man." I have to live up the single life while I can. And even after I meet Mr. Adorable, Satan will find something else to offer on the "Everything You Don't Have" platter. I've decided Satan can keep his platter. I'm good to go.

❤ ❤ ❤ ❤ ❤

I sound very determined and strong and independent and fine in that blog post. But, honestly, singleness has been a continuous battle. I gain a little ground in the war for contentment, but . . . a lonely Friday night happens or another wedding or a good looking guy . . . and then, I'm ravaged and overtaken by dissatisfaction. I've tried everything to overcome these feelings and emotions—most prominently by scouring relationship books for strategies to defeat the woes of singleness.

Therefore, I've probably read at least part of every cutting edge relationship book around. Or if nothing else, I've had my friends explain to me a new insight that they've had after reading the latest Christian relationship book. Let's just say, I'm pretty burnt out on the topic of romantic love.

However, one particular book was swirling around my Bible Study last year and I couldn't seem to avoid it. My friend Kate sprung it on me, and after hearing her rave about it, I couldn't bare the thought of telling her that I didn't want to read it. It had done wonders to help her cope with singleness, but I was pretty sure that I was a hopeless case. Thus, I wrote the following post in order to discreetly vent about my feelings . . .

November 19, 2011

I've never read the entire book *When God Writes Your Love Story*, but I've tried. I read the first chapter or so and decided it was too hard to hear about the wonderful way in which God brought another perfect couple together—because it wasn't happening for me, because I kept messing up. Still my friends continue to recommend this book to me. They love it. I want to love it too . . . but I just want to skip to the end and get the answer to "What the heck do I do in the mean time?"

I've been thinking about this the last few days and some things have come to mind that I want to remember . . . because I completely believe God can write a wicked awesome love story. It's just probably not going to unfold the way it does in the movies or in a Justin Bieber track or even how it did for my best friends.

So, I've compiled a list of things that I want to remember, based on observations of love stories that God has chosen to publish.

#1 When God writes my love story it's going to be perfect for me. Not perfect as in no glitches or hardships—how boring would that be?

#2 I'm going to feel as if God has forgotten to write my love story . . . probably often.

#3 I'm going to make mistakes in the process of living out the story God has written. If I own up to those mistakes and let God have control back, it will make the story He's written even sweeter.

#4 I am going to look foolish. Love, like life, is messy. Sharing crazy moments with friends makes these situations bearable. I know I really appreciate when my friends are honest. Plus, it's nice to know I'm not the only crazy one out there.

#5 Since God has not chosen to publish my romantic love story yet, I don't want to live my life as if it is missing something. It's not.

In all times, I want to pray. I want to pray when I'm happy and thank God for the life I have. When I'm bumming, I want to talk to God about it. It's hard sometimes, but essential, for me to remember that my life already has all the Love I could possibly need in it because I've accepted Jesus as my Savior.

Oh and lastly . . . single ladies, the holidays are not going to be easy. I'm trying to prepare myself. It's the time of year when we see family and friends who all seem to ask, "How are you doing? How is school going? And . . . are you seeing anyone special?" I know that those questions are coming and I want to own them. I want to take those questions as an opportunity to represent the Lord. I want to take on the challenge of being real with them and say that I am single, but that I'm trusting God's timing. It's going to be tough, but only for a few minutes. I know I can't dwell on it. I want to focus on the reason for the season: God's gift to us–Himself in Jesus.

Let the holiday festivities begin!

Lord, please help me to remember these things each day :D

♥ ♥ ♥ ♥ ♥

Please observe how optimistic and chipper I was. Emoticons are so expressive. My readers wouldn't even know how truly repulsed I was by the book. I would definitely say that I had successfully turned my frown upside down. *God would be so proud*, I remember thinking to myself. Looking back, He was probably thinking something else . . .

A month went by and I was really struggling with singleness. It's like an invisible soul-eating plague. The Singleness Plague feasts on the souls of single women who throw themselves pity parties. It even brings its own soundtrack and loves bringing guests to the party. Oh, and the Singleness Plague especially loves reminiscing about your past relationships.

All I can say is take off your party hat and rip down those decorations right now. If you often find yourself sitting in your room playing through perfect scenarios or allowing nostalgia of past princes in your mind, this is a sure symptom of the Singleness Plague. I'm only saying this because I was inflicted by it throughout college. Thankfully, God stepped in . . .

December 16, 2011

I have now read over 150 pages of *When God Writes Your Love Story*, which I bashed in my previous post. Consider me humbled.

It helps to read something prior to making judgments. More precisely, it helps to read something *completely* prior to writing it off.

It's crazy how I came to begin reading *When God Writes Your Love Story* by Eric & Leslie Ludy . . . again. I can honestly say I have no doubt God led me right to it. His timing is nothing short of incredible and ironic. He certainly has a sense of humor.

A few days before heading home for Thanksgiving break, my friend Kate messaged me asking if I still had her copy of *WGWYLS*. Another one of her friends had wanted to read it, but she couldn't find it. I said I was almost positive I had given it back to her.

When I went home for break, I hardly had any down time. One night before bed, the thought occurred to me that I should check my bookshelf to make sure I didn't have Kate's book. I was a little annoyed because I knew I didn't have it, but I thought I could at least prove myself right.

As I scanned the shelf, *WGWYLS* caught my eye. *No way*, I thought as I picked up the book. A card from Kate marked the spot where I had left off near the end of chapter two. As I held the book in my hands, I felt a little nudge of desire . . . I sat down on my bed and began to read.

The words were nothing that I remembered. The bitter taste of my previous experience faded.

In my last post, I said that I couldn't bring myself to read *WGWYLS* because "it was too hard to hear about the wonderful way in which God brought another perfect couple together—because it wasn't happening for me, because I kept messing up."

I now see the gaping flaw in my thinking, the sin in my heart.

Since accepting Jesus as my Savior six years ago, I have slowly given Him control of my life. I trust Him with my future career plans, I trust Him to provide financially, I trust Him to provide friendships and fellowship. I trust Him to take care of my family. I have trusted Him with everything . . . except romantic relationships.

It's been a struggle that I've tried to ignore, conquer, fight, and deny at various times throughout these past few years, but nothing has ever really changed. I've continued in my ways. I would pray . . . but then I would always act on my desires because God didn't seem to be doing anything. Was He not hearing me? Maybe He was just busy. Maybe His silence meant "yes." I would justify doing what I wanted and eventually end up disappointed.

This routine has left me broken-hearted, empty-handed, and pessimistic. It's hard to hope when every time I've liked a guy he's ended up choosing someone else or never making a move, and I just end up embarrassed, confused, and feeling pathetic.

What do those girls have that I don't? What else do I need to do, Lord? I really want this, why aren't you giving it to me!?

Notice a pattern here? It's all about me, getting what I want, when I want it—which is always right now.

I am not sure what exactly spurred the concession, but I can honestly say after six years of writing terrible love stories I am gladly giving God the pen.

One thing that really helped me come to this point was admitting what I was doing was a sin. It was wrong. I could justify my thinking and my actions all day long with reasons that society would adamantly support, but I had been/have been trying to do this part of my life on my own.

It's a sin because I'm not letting the Savior who died for me, live through me . . . at least not completely. 1 Corinthians 6:20 says, "You are not your own, you were bought with a price. So glorify God in your body." I wasn't trusting God or His will for my life. I told Him I was. I truly wanted to, but when the moment came to choose between potentially getting the guy I wanted right now or waiting for the guy God had picked out—I chose "right now" every time.

As I write this, I keep struggling to decide which tense to write in . . . past or present perfect? I wasn't trusting God or I haven't been . . . Past makes it seem as if I wasn't, but am trusting Him now. Present perfect makes it seem as if up until this point, this very moment in time, I haven't been trusting Him. I thought I did at times, I've wanted to always—but now I recognize and confess my sin of trying to rip away the pen from God's hand. I stop myself rather than justifying my actions. I give Him the pen back. I have to go through this give/take multiple times throughout the day, but it's happening less and less.

I'm not done with *When God Writes Your Love Story* quite yet. I'm challenged by it and actually enjoy reading it. Come to find out, it's mostly about letting God's love overflow into all areas of your life rather than tales of perfect Christian couples and desperate single people. God has used this book to transform my mind. Now, I could not be more thankful for the season of singleness, and struggle, that God has allowed me to walk in throughout college. I can't imagine where and with whom I would have ended up had He allowed me to continue in my "right now" seeking ways.

Lord please help me to keep my eyes on You and my ears open to the music you are writing. Help me to appreciate the rests and savor every moment of Your song.

♥ ♥ ♥ ♥ ♥

Maybe I was finally cured of the Singleness Plague. As much I like parties, the singleness pity party was getting really old.

♥ ♥ ♥ ♥ ♥

Part 2

My Favorite Men

I should go into advertising or public relations because if there is someone or something I like, I will promote it like it's the cure for whatever ailment is in your life. If I love you, I want you to love what I love. Consider yourself smitten or else, suffer hearing me talk about it nonstop . . . until you also love it.

My tactics are quite successful. The only problem I've really encountered is converting a select few people into Justin Bieber fans. Honestly, I think that deep down they have accepted him as a talented singer, but are holding out in fear of tarnishing their reputation. I'm trying to be okay with it, but it's just that they are really missing out.

My love for JB started as a fluke. My best friend Sarah was getting married, and I thought I would generate some excitement by selecting a goofy theme song for her wedding. I knew Justin Bieber was known for his over-the-top love songs, so I YouTubed him.

Lo and behold . . . I struck gold! "One Less Lonely Girl" was perfect. After watching the music video, I posted it on Sarah's Facebook wall and it was official. But then, I kept watching it . . . and the more I watched it, the more I liked it. It was so catchy and he was so adorable . . .

My love for Justin was solidified when I went to Asia this past summer. American teenage girls have nothing on Asian girls. One of the first things I learned about my sixteen-year-old Asian students was that they had some serious Bieber Fever. As we sang his songs over and over everywhere we went, most notably at karaoke, I became hooked.

There are so many good memories associated with JB. I know I'm older than he is, but I'm a fan and unashamed. The boy's got skill. If you doubt me, then you must watch the movie *Never Say Never.*

Justin Bieber is a hot topic everywhere, but he's especially controversial in middle and high schools. I discovered during Student Teaching that working him into a lesson is a great way to wake up groggy students. Mention his name and the room will roar as it parts like the Red Sea—fans on one side, haters on the other. Everyone has an opinion about him and everyone wants to share it.

It's crazy how passionate people are about him, which got me thinking . . .

January 14, 2012

Justin Bieber is a powerful name.

People tend to know where they stand on the issue of "him."

I posted a video of Justin visiting an elementary school on Facebook yesterday, followed by, "How can you not love him?" The comments I received were as follows:

2 ladies liked this link.

Male: Boooo!!

Me: Stop sippin Hater-aide:)

Male 2: I'm not sipping the Hater-aide, I'm downing the Hater-aide.

(That received one other male like . . .)

Male 3: Katie, we had a conversation about this. This obsession needs to stop. It's getting out of control and quite frankly he's not even an adult.

Me: Bahaha . . . alright alright . . . but he's such a good person . . .

♥ ♥ ♥ ♥ ♥

Clearly, males are united on this front, as are the ladies. But regardless, I find it very interesting for bigger reasons . . .

♥ ♥ ♥ ♥ ♥

JB makes my list of most influential males in my life right now, along with a few others . . .

Men in My Life that Matter (In Order):
1. Jesus
2. My dad
3. Donald Miller
4. Tim Tebow
5. Justin Bieber

You can see that JB happens to be on the bottom of the list, but you can't fault him. It's a pretty elite group. And probably what I meant is more like, "Men in my life that keep showing up everywhere."

But seriously, our names mean something. They represent who we are, what we are like, because they associate us with something much bigger.

♥ ♥ ♥ ♥ ♥

I read an article about Tim Tebow the other day called "I believe in Tebow." Then I was thinking about what it would be like to be Mrs. Tebow . . .

I decided that it would be way too hard.

Tebow is like Jesus to most people, or at least he represents all they know about Jesus. I don't think he wants that pressure, but he has it.

I was thinking that if I started dating Tim, people would most likely scrutinize my Facebook page, see me holding one red Solo cup, and then proceed to slander my name. They'd probably be upset and say things like . . . "Wow, Tim really settled on this one. He could have any girl in the world and he picked her. Katie Kiesler is so not pretty enough for him . . ."

People are passionate about Tim Tebow. He seems like a good guy who loves Jesus. I respect that . . . and it's nice that his fans and the world want to protect him from unworthy girlfriends.

♥ ♥ ♥ ♥ ♥

Anyway, I know where I stand when it comes to all of these men. I respect them. I love a few of them. But there is only one who I really need to know where I stand when I think about Him or see signs about Him or people bring Him up in conversation.

Jesus Christ.

His name is so powerful that I even get nervous to type it. I know the reaction that His name conjures up when I use it. It's so divisive.

People usually love Him passionately, hate Him passionately, declare their indifference passionately, or wish with a passion that I just wouldn't bring Him up and make them think about "religion" at all.

The thing is, Jesus said some pretty radical stuff. He said, "I am the Road, also the Truth, also the Life. No one gets to the Father apart from me. If you really knew me, you would know my Father as well. From now on, you do know him. You've even seen him!" (John 14:6-7, "The Message")

Basically, Jesus claimed that He was God.

Yep, before you stop reading this just yet, consider this: Jesus was a man born in the Middle East over 2,000 years ago.

Yet, we are still talking about Him today.

I'm going to wrap it up right there. But, I still wonder . . .

Why?

and

Where do you stand when you hear the name Jesus?

♥ ♥ ♥ ♥ ♥

As you can see, I love Jesus and I absolutely adore men that love Jesus too. There are so many great examples out there. One guy whom I would marry in a heartbeat is Donald Miller. That might be a hasty statement, but I am passionate about his writing. He should seriously look into hiring me. I'm telling you, I would be a fantastic publicist. (On a side note, my love for Donald Miller based on his writing could be one reason why I'm fearful of letting others know my thoughts. I'm not sure which is scarier to me, people thinking I'm a weirdo or people thinking that they love me.)

I first stumbled upon Donald Miller's book *Blue Like Jazz* when I was a freshman in college. I was in the bookstore at an Intervarsity Retreat and the title caught my eye. I was positive that I was one of the first to find this gem, but then, when I brought it up in conversation, my friends raved about it too. It was a bit disappointing that I wasn't the trendsetter, but it was nice to have other people to discuss it with.

I re-read *Blue Like Jazz* this past fall and enjoyed it even more than I remembered. Of course, I then had to blog about it . . .

September 31, 2011

I think I could sit here all day reading on this bench with the sun shining down on me, the creek trickling by . . . I'm warm and reading Donald Miller's journey in *Blue Like Jazz*.

My journey has been so messy, but covered up by a layer of plastic perfection. I've only recently realized how wrong I've been in thinking that I can please everyone, read everyone and do what they want. I have to pick one person to please and then be okay if people don't like me. Ugh . . . (Ugh as in . . . gross, I hate not being liked. I am a people pleaser to my core.)

I choose Jesus.

At least I want to.

I have . . . but every part of me does not show it.

What does it look like and sound like to live for Jesus 24/7 . . . not because I have to, but because I love Him with all that I am?

I guess I have to really love Him.

Not for what He can bring me, but for who He is.

Not so that others will like me, because they won't.

I love Jesus (and am loved by Him) so I don't need to gossip to fit in, have everyone like me, do what I think people want me to, or be so concerned with how my life compares to others and I can simply

enjoy

what I've been given.

♥ ♥ ♥ ♥ ♥

When I wrote that post, I had recently begun Student Teaching and was having a hard time figuring out how to be a 22-year-old, a Christian, and a teacher. It was much more difficult than I anticipated to cover up my love for Jesus in the public school system. He was just such an influential part of my life. I didn't want to be slapped with the "Christian" label though. I wanted my fellow teachers and students to know me first. I didn't want to be thrown into the churchy box without a fight.

Donald Miller seemed to be experiencing similar issues in *Blue Like Jazz*. I felt really guilty for not representing Jesus proudly. It was nice to not feel so alone in that struggle. And I'm telling you, once I'm hooked on something or someone there is no stopping the enthusiasm train. Some might say it's borderline obsessive, but I like to think of myself as *passionate.*

At the end of December, while at another Christian conference—this time with CRU, I happened upon Donald Miller's latest book called *A Million Miles in a Thousand Years.* Seriously, it's amazing. You have to read it . . .

January 8, 2011

Donald Miller has become one of my favorite authors. He writes the way that I want to live my life.

Deliberately, but never taking himself too seriously.

Critically, but not cynically.

Honestly, but not to the point that it's TMI.

He's willing to share the uncomfortable, ugly, raw moments of life—not for attention but rather as an opportunity to show how God can use all of it in unexpected ways.

Through reading Donald Miller and knowing others like him, I've realized the most effective writing and living are done when we are willing to be vulnerable. I think we spend most of our lives trying to cover up our insecurities.

I've realized, though, we can either choose to be vulnerable or have moments of vulnerability sneak up on us. Like when you're happily alone, strutting around your house naked, but then hear a sound. Suddenly, the comfort and confidence you felt in your own skin evaporates. You run to the nearest room, hurrying to shut the door. Then you wait, and listen quietly for an opportunity to make an escape. Your mind races trying to think of an excuse for your current nude state. You're embarrassed.

But, if you live your life listening for the Lord, obeying when He asks you to be vulnerable, you never have to worry about being walked in on. Your soul is ready to be seen. And, He won't allow your life to be marked by shame or embarrassment.

I hope you can understand what I mean. Whether we choose to admit it or not, we need each other to share our embarrassing moments, our hurts and our fears. For one, it reminds us that we're normal. It reminds us that we all actually have a lot more in common than not. We don't have to hide. We are who we are.

The good news is: He is who we aren't.

Lord, we all have the same outer shell. Help us to be vulnerable to Your glory.

♥ ♥ ♥ ♥ ♥

Part 3

The Past

I mentioned earlier that I have written some terrible love stories. I spent most of college reliving them, walking back through them, I guess so that along the way God could remove the shards of my old broken heart that remained stuck in my new one. Once I accepted Jesus' love and forgiveness when I was sixteen, I started walking with Him. However, prior to that and even after, I did some serious damage. It was difficult to make a clean break from my old desires and habits.

After one particularly heart-wrenching break-up near the end of my junior year of college, I decided that I would pull a Taylor Swift and crush my ex-boyfriend with lyrics. Then, I realized my guitar playing skills would shame me more than him.

I don't know why, but I really felt the need for him to feel my hurt. I wanted him to be hurting as badly as I was, I think, just so that I didn't feel so stupid. Almost a year after our break-up, I wrote this . . .

Mistakes Haunting Me

Sometimes, most times, when I think back to the people that I loved, the person that I was . . . I feel like I'm reading the pages of a book written about someone else's life. I can't believe that was me. I can't believe that was you. I can't believe there was an *us*.

It's not that I regret it. It just doesn't feel like it happened to me and yet, I can't forget it. I feel like it's still refracting and reflecting back on me, haunting me.

Jesus intercepted my mind, my thoughts, my mistakes, my shame. He's changed me from the inside out. But I'm afraid you still see the stain.

Lord, let them see my heart, look at You and Your still-in-progress work of art. Help us all to look beyond our burned bridges, charred reputations, scattered shards of memories, and gaze at the One who took on the weight of all the hate to find the freedom in redemption that we all crave.

♥ ♥ ♥ ♥ ♥

From there, God took me back even further . . . to the first boy that I let break my heart. Then, I broke his. Then, he died. I thought I was over it, that I had mourned him enough, but last year all the memories came flooding back . . .

Boy #1

Was it your boyish charm,
ripped jeans,
ruggedness,
badass strut
or light easy smile?

Was it your confidence,
your sweetness?
You noticed me.
That's all it took.

I think we were right for each other
at the time.
I was so naïve
at the time.
You were in over your head
Living life with no reason or rhyme.

You lived to please.
You protected me with your lies.
You didn't want to disappoint me
and still after all this time . . .

I can't forget you, I can't put this to rest.
You hurt me so bad, but I could never admit it.
My pride got in the way.
I couldn't let you say, "I'm sorry."
So I withheld the precious gift of forgiveness
and I ran away.

I thought fate would sort it out, clean it up and one day
we would catch up
shoot some hoops and watch Garden State,
understand each other—even though on the outside
our lives were so far away.

Now I look back and wonder-
How did it all get so complicated?
Your lies, my ignorance,
your apologies, my self-righteousness?

Then . . . now . . .
It's too late.
The day you died
I realized the weight
of all the words I left
unsaid.

♥ ♥ ♥ ♥ ♥

I think poor poetry writing skills are excused when you're simply trying to flush out emotions. It felt good to write about him. I needed to find a way to synthesize my emotions into comprehendible words. If I could do that, I knew I could at least preserve a part of him and let go of the part of me that was holding on to the entire situation with fear and guilt.

I had tried in the past to convey verbally to friends what I was going through, but no one really seemed to understand. It wasn't their fault. I don't think I was making any sense.

My thoughts were tangled up in God's proclaimed unchanging goodness, bad things happening to good people I knew, and my inability to take away any of their pain or my own. To cope, I became my own form of Emo. I tried examining life through a microscopic lens, craving understanding of every convoluted detail. Fall semester of my junior year, I wrote this for a class called "The Essay" . . .

Katie Kiesler
November 11, 2009

Trash

Keystone cans everywhere. McDonalds cups, plastic Quillin's bags, group dynamic worksheets, glass. Broken glass. Chunks of black hair—the remnants of a drunken spontaneous act? Vomit. That's just what I wanted to do when I saw it.

I dislike garbage. Around campus it's everywhere. Do people not care? I want to pick it up, but at the same time I don't want to have to. One time, when I was on a walk I just started picking things up. Mostly Keystone cans, which I felt really awkward about because I don't drink and it was three in the afternoon. When I've picked garbage up when I'm with friends, they always think it's really strange. I do it quite often though, feeling weird about it every time.

The strangest part is that I seem to be selective about the trash I pick up. Like I'll always pick up beer cans if I have a bag to put them in. Newspapers and ads are always picked up—regardless of how nasty they look. But other things just depend. I hate picking up granola bar looking wrappers. They just annoy me. I do it anyway because they're shiny and I can't deny that I see them.

I often think how strange this is. Trash is trash right? Why do I desire to pick any of it up? I guess more perplexing to me is why everyone doesn't want to pick it up.

Yes, I often find myself evaluating trash. The trash on the street and sidewalks, the trash in our lives.

Why do we allow trash to sit, fester, blow around, remain? It's everywhere. It takes a simple action to pick up trash, but it takes action. Effort. You might get dirty. You might get a disease. Probably not. But you might get a strange look. For picking up trash that isn't yours . . . strange how strange people think that is.

" . . . but all the broken and dislocated pieces of the universe—people and things, animals and atoms—get properly fixed and fit together in vibrant harmonies."

In order for garbage to be recycled, it has to be set apart from the other garbage. It has to be picked up, but then it has to be sorted—seen as something that could be reused.

It hurts me when I walk by garbage on the street and don't pick it up. It hurts when I do because I can't pick up everything. Plus, people look at me weird. Why am I even trying? I've been recycled. I guess that's getting me through.

There is just so much garbage.

"At one time you all had your backs turned . . ."

I didn't really understand death. The finality of it. The pain of it. I did understand hurt. He was just the first person I ever really let know me. He lied. Big time.

I believed him completely, though.

I wanted to forgive him.

I didn't.

Then, he died and I couldn't.

Jagged pieces of pride, preventing us from repairing that which we broke, or he broke, or she broke. Whatever, it's broken. We've all turned our backs on the task of picking up, the task of mending. It's awkward and takes effort. It takes filing of rough edges, and usually it never is quite smooth enough . . .

" . . . leading the resurrection parade . . ."

Some people live off trash. They have no choice. There, at the landfill, they find their food, with trash they make their shelter. I wonder if they consider it "trash." I think I would call it something else.

They have no choice though. Their job is sorting through trash. They sort through it, hoping to find something to recycle.

A fresh start. A new use. A second chance to be used.

" . . . towering far above everything, everyone."

We are so immersed in trash that we probably don't even recognize everything that is trash. A fish doesn't know that it's wet. There is so much hurt, so many jagged broken pieces of glass in our life. How often do we just walk over it and allow it to pierce our skin, and then instead of removing it, allow it to slice deeper, to nestle in between our flesh and veins, surrounded by our blood which is working so hard to give us life.

Maybe it will make its way out on its own. Or more likely, it will get lodged in deeper and contaminate everything else.

It takes Someone removed from a situation to see things clearly.

Retrospect, that works too . . . but often too late.

" . . . put your lives together, whole . . ."

I'm pretty sure we don't want to live in and among trash. All around us there is beauty, but we allow trash to infiltrate the beauty. One Keystone can here, a McDonald's cup here, one broken relationship there, a failure just over there . . .

There will always be trash.

I hate that.

I'll always screw up.

I'll always break what He mends.

But He mends, He creates.

It doesn't make sense. I can't comprehend it, but I know it's true.

As I go throughout life, I know God is good and has a plan but what I don't know is what it's going to take to make me truly believe this, where God is going to take me so that I am confident in this belief. I know that Jesus is going to be leading me though . . .

When I hear the name Jesus, I usually picture a Norwegian man holding a lamb. Brown, flowy locks of silky hair—and I am perplexed by the amazing hygiene in the first century. However, on one of my many walks around campus, I thought of what Jesus, who is God yet who came to Earth, must think of all this trash. I thought of all the trash in my life. I wondered how He decided what trash to pick up. Why are some people hurting, while others appear to have a super spiffy life? But then I remembered . . .

I was flying back from Denver. There were so many questions in my mind, so many uncertainties. Life is so uncertain. I looked out the window and noticed a cloud that was darkening one large area. Everywhere else there was sunshine. Jesus used that to show me that I have no idea what's to come. I may be under the clouds, but sunshine is coming. Or, I may be in sunshine I guess . . . which means clouds may be coming. Either way, it is only from way up in the sky that we can see what's next. God is the only one who sits high enough to know what is heading our way. Basically, the Lord so lovingly showed me how ridiculous it is for me to try to figure out my life from the ground. I can only see so far in front of me. He has the best seat in the house and He is willing to lead me in the right direction. I just have to ask and trust Him—it's foolish for me not to. I definitely needed a diagram to understand it. I'm sure I'll fall back into trying to run my life from the ground, but He's so patient.

He's got a supreme seat, far above everything. He is supreme. He delights in picking up trash. I definitely don't understand it . . . but at the same time I think I understand why He can't resist it. Our trash is His soon to be masterpiece. Our darkness could be made into light. A clean slate, a clean sidewalk. What He makes out of us is better than what we were before, there's no way it can't be.

When I was driving this morning, I noticed how clean the sidewalks were. Did anyone else see how beautiful the pavement looked? Probably not. I wouldn't have either had I not been obsessing about trash. We only realize the absence of something after we've been immersed in it.

We're looking at the back of a cross-stitch. Thread all jumbled together—a real crappy mess. On the other side, it's clearly a picture. It all makes sense. It just depends on what side you're looking from. If I'm honest, I know I can't possibly see the beauty on my own.

"He was supreme in the beginning and—leading the resurrection parade—He is supreme in the end. From beginning to end He's there, towering far above everything, everyone. So spacious is He, so roomy, that everything of God finds its proper place in Him without crowding. Not only that, but all the broken and dislocated pieces of the universe—people and things, animals and atoms—get properly fixed and fit together in vibrant harmonies, all because of His death, His blood that poured down from the cross. You yourselves are a case study of what He does. At one time you all had your backs turned to God, thinking rebellious thoughts of Him, giving Him trouble every chance you got. But now, by giving Himself completely at the Cross, actually dying for you, Christ brought you over to God's side and put your lives together, whole and holy in His presence."

-Colossians 1:18-23, "The Message"

Plastic bags, paper bags, leftovers. Things. Some identifiable, some not. Everything old and filthy. Dirty. The discarded remnants of humanity. Trash. It's what pickers of the landfill survive on. They search for anything that can be recycled. They turn it into the government for a little pay. This is their life day after day.

I kind of envy them.

♥ ♥ ♥ ♥ ♥

I like this piece, but it's one of those things that makes perfect sense and doesn't all at the same time. It reminds me of a lava lamp that my grandparents used to have in their living room. Once you flip the switch, the lava just floats whichever way it pleases. My thoughts kind of seem like that. Floating along, seeing the shores of God, but not willing to be anchored by Him. I didn't even know it, but I was struggling. I was in the midst of a personal war. I spiraled into a depression soon after.

April 14, 2011

Sometimes I think that some people can see in me the ugly that I can't see. They say they want to know me, the "real" me, but I'm terrified that if they did, they would be disappointed.

It would be like if they bought a product based on the commercials, based on what the label says it is, based on the picture on the box, only to get it home, open it up and realize

it's not what they thought it was.

You see I think that some people can see right through me. They see the emptiness that I try so hard to hide. They see right through me, they're not impressed by my bubbly personality, they think it's superficiality.

And if I'm honest, I know they're right . . . Because I don't know if I'm right with God, I don't know if sometimes I do nice things in order to play God, in order to avoid God, to look like His angel but to only be a figurine.

I've never thought that I could be a lie. But I also never let anyone else get close enough to open my inner box. The one that is shoved so far down inside of me, I forget that it's there. I don't even know if I have the key, I don't think I want anyone to know the combination, even me.

It's scary to admit that there is an outside that you all see, a person that society, my family, and me believe to be a Christian, believe to have a purpose, believe to be a true friend, a leader, but me, I might just be a trend.

If you saw the real me, if I gave God the key, if I let Him tear down the walls, fight the fear, devour my insecurities, let down my hair, tear down the curtain that's holding me up, will I still be able to stand? Will you want me as your friend?

God if you really can make a new heart in me, I give you permission to throw away the nothingness, that inner part of me that has never existed, yet I insisted unknowingly to rule me, then just maybe I will be whole. I'll know that I'm wholly unworthy and that will be okay. I won't try to hide it and work my way to You. I'll be able to be still and rest completely in You, in me.

♥ ♥ ♥ ♥ ♥

All of my experiences up to this point have shown me that if I don't give up the pen and let God write the story of my life, just glancing in the mirror is overwhelming. I'm a perfectionist, so I want every detail to be flawless, every line spoken to be impeccable.

I didn't realize it at the time, but I was trying to be God's poster child. In every area of my life, I didn't want to let anyone down. I thought my job was to get the envy of my friends and family so that they thought to themselves, "Wow, her life is so wonderful. Nothing bad ever happens to her . . . I want to know her God so my life can be perfect too."

I was especially determined to win God and the world's equivalent of an Academy Award for Best Romantic Comedy. This ambition was the catalyst for many awkward relationships, extreme disenchantment, hours spent learning how to play guitar, and preoccupation with past mistakes.

Eventually, God allowed all of this anxiety and obsessing about perfection to crush me. I'm sure, in hopes that I would stop trying so hard and start living a life of joy with Him as writer, producer, director, and leading Man. Lyrics spilled out of me as I started meeting men who actually loved me like their sister in Christ . . .

All I knew how to do was argue with you.
And all I ever wanted was someone to run to.
I'm sorry that I pushed you away,
But you showed me how much I can gain.

Now I'm realizing and I'm healing.
You're showing me the way.

That there's a love that's bigger than
My complicated maze of hurts and problems.
There's a love that's stronger than
All my broken ties
And you're in this for more than just a temporary prize.

And I can't thank you enough
For your understanding eyes.
You're representing Jesus
And now I know that He's alive.

All I knew how to do was argue with you.
And all I wanted was someone to run to.

Part 4

The Future

January 17, 2012

As I put my key into the door of the Challenge Reading classroom at O Middle School for one of the last times, I realized that my key chain was shrinking. I found the key for the door with amazing speed, without fumbling through the mess of annoyingly similar shapes.

In the last two days, I've shed the two keys to church, my apartment key, and in a few days will be getting rid of the remaining three classroom keys and two building fobs.

My life was gradually wrapped up by threads of commitment and opportunity this past semester, and in what seems like an instant, it is unraveling.

Soon, all that will remain is my car key on the once blinged out, but now rusty "K" key chain that my mom bought me for Christmas last year.

My safe comfortable college life in La Crosse, where I have now lived for four and a half years, is coming to an end. My story with predictable plot elements is now reaching its resolution, which feels more like a cliffhanger.

I'm not sure how I feel about all of the unknowns . . . this world where nothing is known. I keep picturing a blank white page. If I were a painter, it'd be a bare canvas where beautiful colors would eventually be splashed. But, I'm an English teacher. So, life is just an empty Word document with a blinking cursor impatiently staring me in the face, waiting for me to make a decision, to make a statement.

I don't want to simply dream and write about what I want my life to be. I truly have no ideas. I have things that I think would be cool like writing a book, being on the Ellen Show, traveling all over the world, teaching overseas, meeting the love of my life . . . but they probably sound better in my head.

Real life is messy and hard and never turns out like I've imagined. Usually it's better. So, I try not to dream but rather to pray. If there is one thing I know, it's that I have no clue what I want. I'm fickle. I'm picky. And I'm scared of a lot of things. Especially commitment.

Committing to one of my crazy fantasies, I'm pretty sure would be comparable to cliff diving. All of my ideas seem great, but they are most likely just fun to say to other people so that you can hear them talk about how interesting your life is. Cliff diving really impresses people.

My friend Adrienne went to South Africa and jumped off a bridge that was 216 meters high, which doesn't sound that high in meters because as Americans we can't convert the metric system. However, I learned that it's 709 feet high. I was impressed when I saw the video of her jumping and was even more impressed when I Googled "Bloukrans Bungy."

I want my life to be like that.

But a jump only lasts a few seconds, or minutes if you're really brave . . .

I want God to write an incredible story, where He makes a bridge over steep mountains and beautiful rivers and He lays down His coat over oceans so my feet don't get wet and holds out His hand like a true gentleman to help me over each one and we enjoy each others' company so much that we don't care who sees us or is impressed by how cute we are. I want my life to be filled with the dialogue of people that I've never met yet, and conversations over coffee with old friends. I want to give God my car key and I want to take the risk of living with no keys at all.

God, I'm going to need some serious help.

♥ ♥ ♥ ♥ ♥

The weird thing about journaling or publishing a blog is that so often when I re-read what I've written, I feel like it's hitting me for the first time. I sometimes don't even recall writing the words that are now speaking to me. It's just like when I worked one summer as a youth missions camp counselor and had to give my testimony each week. I found that when God was speaking through me, He was speaking to me.

I like to re-read what I've written. Not to dwell on how great it sounds, but to be reminded of the lesson that God worked so hard to teach me. It's crazy how quickly I forget . . .

October 18, 2011

Driving home tonight, I was listening to WWIB. A sermon by Greg Laurie was airing. "Have you ever left your First Love?" he asked.

I cringed.

He went on to ask, "What happened when you did? King David left his First Love when he became fixated on Bathsheba. We know how that story ends . . ."

I can relate . . . Relationships were present in the times when I most obviously left my First Love. I became fixated on obtaining, pleasing, and keeping them. I don't want to do that again.

Although it's easy to blame boys, other things that seem "good" have drawn me away as well. Teaching has stolen my time, even ministry has romanced me. It seems ridiculous that I could fall in love with those things. They are a weak replacement for God. They only take, they never give. They leave me drained and bitter and empty. I thought they gave me an identity. Really they just gave me something to do for a while.

Also, when I was thinking about how the idea of God as our First Love compares to human relationships I realized . . . If I love someone I desire to spend time with them. I care about what they say. In the same way, if I truly love God I will desire to spend time with Him, doing the things He loves. I'll take Him into consideration when making decisions. I'll slip Him into conversations just to say

His name. I'll trust Him. Out of respect, I won't do the things He hates. I definitely won't cheat on Him with cheap imitations when I get bored or can't see Him at work in my life.

Greg Laurie gave me a lot of good stuff to think about.

I'm still working out all the details.

Heavenly Father, teach me how to love You better as my First Love. Don't let me leave You.

♥ ♥ ♥ ♥ ♥

This is still my prayer today, or at least it needs to be . . . I'm 22 and single.

♥ ♥ ♥ ♥ ♥

Epilogue

There are very few things I'm sure of when it comes to what I want to do with my life, but I've got a couple passions nailed down. First of all, I have this relentless desire to connect people. I love meeting someone new, finding out where they went to school, what they like, what they want, and then introducing them to someone or something that could help them achieve a goal or pursue their passion.

If there were a profession where I could be a platonic matchmaker, I'd do it. And not to brag, but I'd be really good at it, probably for no other reason than no one else in the world would be crazy enough to think that Platonic Love Matchmaking was a sensible business ploy.

But that is what I want to do. I want to connect people to other people and other things that they didn't know they needed. I want to be connected too.

I think writing is one way that connections become apparent, but it's a risk. People can reject your writing, which means they are rejecting your thoughts, which makes it feel like they are rejecting you . . .

I also adore middle and high school students. Yes, as a teacher they drive you crazy sometimes, but I love being around them.

I just finished a semester long internship a few days ago, and I can't stop thinking about how much I'm going to miss those kids.

Right before I left, I completed a poetry unit with my seventh graders. They definitely hated poetry and told me so multiple times. But, despite their loathing of the subject, the coolest thing happened. We held our own poetry slam and they threw down some awesome spoken word.

One day, in the midst of feeling like a cool hipster teacher, it hit me: I was being completely unfair. If I was going to ask my students to perform a poem, I probably needed to participate in the poetry slam as well.

I wrote my poem in ten minutes when I was home over Christmas break. The words came to me as I was trying to find ways to avoid family tasks and cleaning. I didn't think that it would be the poem I would perform, but I didn't have anything else so I ended up using it.

As my students seemed to notice, sharing something that you've written in front of a live audience, about a topic you choose, is intimidating. Most wrote about their favorite season or sport or poetry itself, but regardless of their topic, I saw a part of their soul that they hadn't shown before. It was amazing.

I was especially nervous to perform. I was supposed to be the one who knew what she was doing. I was uneasy, though, because what I had written was personal. I didn't want it to get weird. Would they judge me? Would they still think I was cool—if they even ever did?

Yes, I was butterflies-in-stomach sick over what my seventh grade students would think of my one-minute poem. It went like this . . .

This is Your Notice, Proceed

I just want to be known.

I don't want to be famous.
I don't need a lot of money, fans, the spotlight . . .

I just don't want to be alone.

I want to be known
    and
    noticed
        and
        found.

Sometimes my feet are inches off the ground,
But that's not far enough.

No one seems to notice.

People just pass me by.

Glancing, but never making an effort
    to stop
        reverse
           and say
               "That's pretty high."

Hi . . . hello!
Could I really be this simple,
           this ordinary?
Who's to say that I can't become
           extraordinary?

Take the time to see me,
the person standing next to you.
Don't let society's fast paced
                    never caring
                    cold hearted
                    greed and need
                    to succeed
                                        get the best of you.

I want to believe the best in you.
But you have to try too.

Show me that you have some left in you.

Even if I'm hundreds or thousands of miles away,
I'm not too good for you.

I'm just breaking free of you.

I'm starting fresh and starting again.
I'm going to astound, astonish, and offend.
I'm offending the norm
                          the culture
                          the known.

And the next time
I'm standing next to you,

You'll know.

♥ ♥ ♥ ♥ ♥

I screwed up. I forgot to say a line, but I don't think anyone could tell. It felt really good to be so real. I guess it was liberating to say what I had wanted to shout to my family, friends, and God for a long time—even if it was only in front of thirty-one seventh grade students and my cooperating teacher. It was a rush.

I want everyday of my life to be like that. I want people to know who I actually am as a 22-year-old, not who I was.

I used to be shy and quiet.

No one believes me now, but my grandma will tell you.

When I am in my hometown, I feel like everyone expects me to be my old self. Most of the time I concede and jump into my quiet shy girl box. People like that girl.

It's hard not to. She doesn't say much.

She doesn't ruffle any feathers.

She doesn't voice her opinion.

She doesn't show emotion.

This 22 & single girl makes a lot more noise.

katiesjournal.org

Afterword

I feel like I'm finally getting the hang of this whole being 22 and single thing. It's awesome.

Unfortunately, 10 days from now, everything will change . . .

♥ ♥ ♥ ♥ ♥

On February 17, I'll no longer be 22 . . . and I'm already mourning the loss of the number that I've grown to love.

It sounds silly to think that I could fall in love with a number, but 22 has seen me through a year of events unlike any other.

We've bonded through times that were exhilarating, terrifying, painful, sad, and precious . . .

It was exhilarating to navigate four European countries in six days with two girlfriends. (We survived only by the sweet grace of God.)

It was terrifying to think about graduating college with my relationship status set to "single."

It was painful to experience God scooping the selfishness from my soul and scraping off the prideful scum around my heart.

It was sad to leave my friends, ministry, and students that had become my family.

It was precious to see so many of my sweet friends marry the person that God had so clearly planned for them.

♥ ♥ ♥ ♥ ♥

The number 22 is now so dear to me that I can hardly resist the urge to take a picture every time I see it.

It's like knowing that in just a few days I'm going to have to say good-bye to a beloved friend who, although I don't want to admit it, I'll never see again.

I want to cherish every moment that I have with it from here on out.

22 will forever be inscribed in my journal as the year that God strengthened me through struggles and then showered me with surprises, putting His unfathomable goodness on display.

I guess what I'm trying to say is that 22 has been Manasseh and Ephraim . . .

Manasseh: "God has made me forget all my hardship in my father's house."

Ephraim: "God has made me fruitful in the land of my affliction."

Like with all words that gain immense significance in my life, I am now considering getting Manasseh and Ephraim as tattoos. (Don't tell my Dad:))

Compiling *22 & Single,* and possibly publishing it as a real live book that I can hold in my hands, has made me forget all my previous hardships. They are no longer holding me in shame. In fact, I treasure them.

Having the opportunity to share my thoughts through my blog has made everything I've gone through these past few years worth it. God has truly made my life fruitful when it was once filled with affliction.

Now, because I can so clearly see God's providence, I'm beginning to warm up to the idea of turning 23.

It's just that change is really hard for me. I'm so bad at processing . . . and a new number changes everything . . .

I'm going to have to remember to write "23" on all official documents, memorize that my age is "23" so that if I ever get questioned by police I don't make myself look drunk or guilty, and I'm going to have to practice saying "23" out loud so that I can sound convincing and confident when my students ask how old I am. Yes, a lot is about to change . . .

Except of course . . . .

my relationship status.

♥ ♥ ♥ ♥ ♥

Lord, I love the story of Joseph these days. Thank you for dragging me into the Old Testament, despite my resistance. I now cherish Joseph's words in Genesis 50:20, "You intended to harm me, but God intended it for good to accomplish what is now being done . . ." Most times, I ignorantly welcomed harmful things into my life. I created them. I desired them. You have redeemed my mistakes. You deserve all the glory for any good that comes from me.

♥ ♥ ♥ ♥ ♥

Good-bye 22. It's been fun, but this is what I want now . . .

I want to be known as the 23 year-old who is foolishly in love with a Prince she can't see. I want to rejoice while holding the rose of singleness, even when my hands bleed from its thorns. I want to resist the urge to envy the pairs growing in the middle of my neighbors' gardens. I want to be rooted in the simple truth that unripe pairs taste like lies and lingering loneliness. I want to put Jesus on my bullet wound and cling to His heart wrenching hope because He was kind enough to be a Band-Aid when He should have stayed a King.

I can't wait to fall in love with the number 23 . . .

Acknowledgements

Thanking everyone who has made *22 & Single* possible is like trying to thank everyone who has made a positive impact on my life.

There are so many. Thank you to the 50 people who backed me with donations and helped me successfully fund my Kickstarter project. God used you to make this happen. Without you taking a leap of faith, my dream of being an author would most likely have gone unrealized. You have given me confidence and motivation throughout this entire process.

Thank you to my friends and family. I have been and continue to be so incredibly blessed by your presence in my life. God has overwhelmed me with His love, grace, and kindness—which shines through you.

Mom, thank you for always taking such good care of me. I especially appreciated you reminding me to eat while working on this project—and forcing me to when I would forget. Dad, thank you for taking on the challenge of communicating with two daughters. I respect you more than you will ever know. Kristi, thank you for going through life first. You have taught me so much. I love getting to know you not only as my sister, but also as my best friend.

Lastly, thank you Jesus—the author and perfecter of my faith. You've given me life. You've put up with my craziness. You've never given up on me. My life is Yours.

Printed in the United States
By Bookmasters